LAO ZI's POEMS

(large print)

The Way of Nature

and

The Way of People

Dr. Auke Schade

nemonik-thinking.org

Copyright

First Edition 24-02-2018
@ nemonik-thinking.org
ISBN 978-0-473-43181-5

Free eBook @
nemonik-thinking.org

Abstract

The Chinese philosopher Lao Zi wrote two-and-halve thousand years ago the brilliant book *Dao De Jing*, which means literally—*A Classic about the Way of Nature and the Way of People*. That ancient book contains eighty-one poems of extraordinary depth describing a natural way of living that provides long-term success with minimum effort—*The Way of Nature has no favourites. It is always with the competent people [79]*. The theme of his poems is to maximize your success, which is to *obtain what you seek and escape what you suffer [62]*. You maximize your success by aligning the *Way of People* with the *Way of Nature—Have a long life through a lasting regard for the Way [59]*. Manmade climate change is only one of many consequences of ignoring Lao Zi's wisdom. His superb poems form a bridge across the deep fault lines that are created and maintained by nationality, ideology, religion, race, and greed. The present book comprises an extract from (Schade, Lao Zi's Dao De Jing Demystified, 2017, pp. Meta-translation version).

Contents

Yin-Yang

LAO ZI'S DAO DE JING

老子之道德經

The Way of Nature

and

The Way of People

Dr. Auke Schade

THE ART OF LIVING

More than two-and-halve thousand years ago, the Chinese philosopher Lao Zi wrote the famous book *Dao De Jing*, which means literally—*A Classic about the Way of Nature and the Way of People*. It contains a collection of eighty-one mysterious poems about the art of living a long and effortless life. For that reason, Lao Zi defines success in life as—*Obtaining what you seek and escaping what you suffer [62]*. You maximize your success by aligning the *Way of People* with the *Way of Nature—Have a long life through a lasting regard for the Way [59]*.

Lao Zi's biography was included by the historian Ssu-ma-Ch'ien (145-90 BC) in the *Shih Chi* or *Historical Records,* which comprises the first comprehensive history of China. He suggested that Lao Zi's real name was Li Erh, who was a historian in the former state Chu.

However, that information might be spurious, because *Shih Chi* was written about four hundred years after Lao Zi's death. In accord, Fung Yu Lan raised questions about Lao Zi's identity (Bodde, 1983, pp. 170-171).

Legend has it that Lao Zi left Chu because of the corruption in that state. Travelling through a narrow mountain pass, the keeper of that pass asked him to write down his wisdom. During one night, Lao Zi wrote *Dao De Jing*. It might be that the pass refers to the transformation from life to death and that he wrote the manuscript during the last days of his life.

There are doubts whether Lao Zi generated the ideas expressed in *Dao De Jing*. Some scholars suggest that Lao Zi's sayings were widely known in China during that time, while others question whether he wrote the book at all. Indeed, Lao Zi does not claim to be the creator of those ideas.

Lao Zi refers to the *Ancients*, or the sages of antiquity, as the source of his wisdom—*Those Ancients who practised the Way competently, understood profoundly the smallest details [15]. So, why did the Ancients value the protection of the Way? Did they not say: "Use it to obtain what you seek and use it to escape what you suffer [62]." Therefore, the Ancients said: "Do not use the Way of Action to enlighten people [65]." That is called matching with nature. It is the ultimate principle of the Ancients [68].* This suggests that the wisdom in *Dao De Jing* is much older than two-and-halve thousand years, which makes it even more mysterious.

The present book comprises an English translation of Lao Zi's manuscript that is extracted from (Schade, Lao Zi's Dao De Jing Demystified, 2017, pp. Meta-translation version).

DAO – THE WAY OF NATURE

Poems 1-37

01

The Way that can be discussed
is not the eternal Way.
The name that can be named
is not the eternal name.
Nameless: it is the origin of All-things.
Being Named: it is the Mother of All-things.

Be always without desires and see its details.
Have always desires and see its limits.
These two things occur together.
Different names with the same meaning.
Profoundly mysterious,
they are the gateway to many details.

02

If everyone in the world
recognises beauty as beautiful,
then there is already ugliness.
If everyone
recognizes good as goodness,
then there is already badness.

Existence and Non-existence
generate each other.
Difficult and easy turn into each other.
Long and short shape each other.
High and low fill each other.
Tone and voice harmonise each other.
Before and after follow each other forever.

Sages manage their affairs with Non-action.
They carry out their teachings
without speaking.

All-things rise, but do not initiate.
Act, but do not rely on it.
Succeed, but do not claim.
Only that what is not claimed
can therefore not be taken away.

03

Do not value knowledge
and the people will not strive.
Do not admire goods
that are difficult to obtain
and the people will not steal.
Do not display
what is desirable
and the people will not revolt.

Therefore, sages rule by
emptying the minds of people,
filling their stomachs,
weakening their ambitions,
and strengthening their bones.

Let the people always be
without knowledge and without desire.
Let those who know,
not dare to act but stop.
Act with Non-action,
then there will be no anarchy.

04

The Way is empty,
but use it and it has not to be refilled.
It is so deep!

Like the Ancestor of All-things;
it smoothens their blending;
untangles their disorder;
softens their glare;
and merges their dust.

Invisible.
Nevertheless, it seems to exist.
I do not know whose child it is,
but it seems to predate the Emperor.

05

The Sky and the Earth
do not have to be benevolent
if All-things would act as straw dogs.
Sages do not have to be benevolent
if common people
would act as straw dogs.

What is between the Sky and the Earth
is like a pair of bellows.
It is empty, but not exhausted.
Use it and more will be produced.

Listening to many details is exhausting
and not as good as following your heart.

06

The Immortal Valley Spirit
is called the Mysterious Female.
The home of this Mysterious Female
is called the origin of the Sky and the Earth.
It seems to exist forever
and using it is no hard work.

07

The Sky endures and the Earth last long.
Why do the Sky and the Earth
last long and endure?
That is, because they do not
foster themselves.
Therefore, they can live long.

Accordingly, sages withdraw themselves.
Yet they are first.
They put themselves outside.
Yet they are inside.
Because they are selfless,
therefore, their self-interest is fulfilled.

08

Superior goodness is like water.
The goodness of water benefits All-things
and it does not strive.
It occupies places everybody dislikes.
Therefore, it is close to the Way.

In dwelling, the goodness is location.
In thinking, the goodness is depth.
In giving, the goodness is benevolence.
In speaking, the goodness is truth.
In ruling, the goodness is order.
In working, the goodness is skill.
In action, the goodness is timing.

Only those who do not strive
will therefore not fail.

09

Accumulating and filling up
are not as good as stopping in time.
Hammer it too sharp and it cannot last long.

A room filled with gold and jade
cannot be defended competently.
Admiring wealth and arrogance
brings personal loss and misfortune.

When merit is achieved,
withdrawing yourself
is the Way of Nature.

10

Carry the team spirit
and unite it inseparable with the One.
Concentrate vital energy
and be as flexible as an infant.
Study and eliminate problems.
Inspect them competently without flaws.

Love the people and rule the country
without using knowledge.
Open and close the gates
of nature as a female.
Understand the surroundings
without using knowledge.

Generate them and raise them.
Generate, but do not possess.
Develop but do not exploit.
This is called profound virtue.

11

Thirty spokes merge into one hub,
but its Non-existence
is useful for a carriage.
Moulded clay makes a cup,
but the Non-existence of clay
is useful for a cup.
Chiselled doors and windows make a room,
but their Non-existence
is useful for a room.
Therefore, using Existence is beneficial,
while using Non-existence is useful.

12

The five colours will blind people's eyes.
The five tones will deafen people's ears.
The five flavours will refresh people's mouth.

Galloping and hunting in the field
will madden people's minds.
Goods that are difficult to obtain
will harm people.
Therefore, sages will rule for the stomach
and not for the eyes.
Therefore, reject that and accept this.

13

Favour and disgrace are just like distress.
They cause great suffering just like the body.

Why saying that favour and disgrace
are just like distress?
Favour is inferior.
Receiving it is like distress
and losing it is like distress.
Whether it is called favour or disgrace,
it is like distress.

Why saying that it cost great suffering
just like the body?
Why do I have great suffering?
That is, because I have a body.
If I had no body, how could I suffer?

Therefore, those who purposely
value their body for serving the world
can be entrusted
with the purpose of the world.
Those who purposely
love their body for the world
can be entrusted with the world.

14

Look at it, yet it cannot be seen.
Its name is called invisible.
Listen to it, yet it cannot be heard.
Its name is called inaudible.
Seize it, yet it cannot be caught.
Its name is called insubstantial.
These three phenomena
cannot be extensively evaluated,
because they merge into the One.
Above the One there is no void.
Below it there is no substance.
It is infinite.
It cannot be named.
Every time it returns to Nothingness.
It is called shapeless.
Like the shape of Nothingness.
It is called dim and elusive.
Face it, yet you do not see its head.
Follow it, yet you do not see its back.

Adhere to the present Way
in order to manage the present Existence.
Use it to understand its ancient origin.
That is called the principle of the Way.

15

Those Ancients who practised
the Way competently,
understood profoundly the smallest details.
Their depth cannot be known.
They cannot be understood.

Therefore, they are difficult to describe
and called:
"Careful, like they were
wading through a river in the winter.
Hesitant, like they were
afraid of their surrounding neighbours.
Solemn, like they were guests.
Dissipating, like they were melting snow.
Vague, like they were simple.
Empty, like they were a valley.
Merging, like they were mud."

Do not stir mud
and it will slowly clear.
If settled, stir it
and then it will slowly come alive.

Those who keep the Way
do not desire fullness.
Only those who desire no fullness
are therefore able
to exhaust themselves without renewal.

16

Concentrate on removing extremes.
Nurture tranquillity diligently.
All-things around us rise,
and I watch them return.
Those things are numerous
and each one returns to its roots.

Returning to the roots is called tranquillity.
Tranquillity is called returning to order.
Returning to order is a constant.
Knowing this constant is brilliant.
Not acknowledging this constant is arrogant.
Arrogance causes misfortune.

Knowing this constant is embracing.
Embracing is honourable.
Honourable is Kingly.
Kingly is natural.
Natural is the Way.
The Way is forever.
It produces a life without danger.

17

Great leaders are those known
by their subjects to exist.
Next are those who are loved and praised.
Next are those who are feared.
Next are those low ones who are insulting.
If there is not enough trust,
then there is distrust.

Those of value speak about their plans
and succeed in completing their affairs.
Yet, the common people will say;
it happened naturally.

18

If the great Way is rejected,
then there will be benevolence and justice.
Knowledge and cleverness will appear
and then there is great hypocrisy.
Family relationships will be disharmonious
and then there is animal dirt everywhere.
The State's household
will be a confused disorder and
then there is bureaucracy.

19

Discard adoration and reject knowledge
and the people will benefit a hundred times.
Discard benevolence and reject righteousness
and the people will return to
filial piety and compassion.
Discard cleverness and reject profit
and there will be no burglars and thieves.

These three declarations
could be regarded to be inadequate slogans.
Therefore, let the people have institutions.
Show modesty and embrace simplicity.
Lack selfishness and restrain desires.
Discard knowledge and there are no worries.

20

Flattery and rebuke:
how much do they differ from each other?
Satisfaction and dissatisfaction:
how much do they differ from each other?

What everybody fears, one has to fear as well.
Everybody stares at me.
They do not stop.
Everybody is very happy.
Just like a big sacrificial feast in the village
and stepping on stage in the springtime.

I am quiet and not predictable.
Just like a baby that has not coughed yet.
Tired; without a place to return to.
Everybody has a surplus.
Yet, only I seem to be lacking.

I am a very stupid fool
in other people's minds.
Everybody is very clear.
Only I seem to be confused.
Everybody is very certain.
Only I seem to be very uncertain.

They are indifferent.
It is like staring at the sea.
It is like having no place to rest.

Everybody has a purpose.
Only I am stubborn
and my purpose seems to be ridiculous.
I desire only to differ from other people
and value the nourishment from the Mother.

21

The greatest virtue
is following only the Way.
The contents of the Way
are only elusive and dim.

Dim. Elusive.
Inside there are images.
Elusive. Dim.
Inside there are things.
Hidden. Obscure.
Its centre has energy.
Its energy is very real.
Inside it, there is information.

From past to present times,
its name was never erased.
Therefore, align
with the Father of the Multitude.
How do I know
that the Father of the Multitude is like this?
From this account.

22

Bend then be preserved.
Twist then be straightened.
Empty then be filled.
Exhaust then be renewed.
Lack then receive.
Have surplus then be confused.
Therefore, sages hold on to the One.
Accordingly, they are the shepherds
of the world.

They do not display themselves.
Therefore, they are brilliant.
They do not regard themselves.
Therefore, they are honoured.
They do not boast about themselves.

Therefore, they have merit.
They are not arrogant.
Therefore, they will develop.
They do not strive.
Therefore, no one can strive with them.

The ones called the 'Ancients' said:
"Those who bend will be preserved."
Is that saying insignificant?
However, true preservation was their return.

23

Speaking seldom is natural.
Strong storms do not drum all morning.
Violent rains do not drum all day.
Who serves them?
The Sky and the Earth.
Yet, they cannot go on forever.
So how about people?

Therefore, those who submit
their affairs to the Way
will merge with the Way.
Those who submit
their affairs to virtue
will merge with virtue.
Those who submit

their affairs to loss
will merge with loss.

Those who merge with virtue
will also gain the Way.
Those who merge with loss
will also lose the Way.

24

Those who stand on tiptoe
do not stand firm.
Those who display themselves
are without brilliance.
Those who regard themselves
are without honour.
Those who boast about themselves
are without merit.
Those who are arrogant
are without development.

Their Way is called:
"Leftover food and unnecessary action."
These things are disgusting.
Therefore, those who have desires
will not succeed.

25

There was a thing Undivided and complete
before the Sky and the Earth were born.
Desolate. Empty.
Independent and unchanging.
Yet, it acts as the origin of the world.

I do not know how its name is pronounced,
but I call it the Way.
If I were forced to describe it,
then I would call it great.
Great means continuous.
Continuous means forever.
Forever means returning.

Therefore, the Way is great;
the Sky is great;
the Earth is great;
and the King is also great.
Inside the universe there are four Greatnesses
and the King is one.
Therefore, people follow the Earth;
the Earth follows the Sky;
the Sky follows the Way;
and the Way follows nature.

26

Heaviness is the foundation of lightness.
Tranquillity is the sovereign of rashness.
Therefore, great men who travel all day
will not leave their heavy wagons.
Although, there is a walled guest house
in a quiet place nearby, they remain aloof.

Just like a lord with ten thousand chariots
who considers himself less important
than the State.
Lightness will lose the foundation.
Rashness will lose the sovereign.

27

Competent travellers
leave no trail.
Competent speakers
pursue no flaws.
Competent accountants
do not use bamboo counting sticks.
Competent wardens
lock without keys.
Yet, it cannot be opened.
Competent weavers
arrange without strings.
Yet, it cannot be untied.

Sages save people always competently
by not rejecting them.
Not rejected things are resources.
Accordingly, that is called brilliant.

Therefore, competent people
are the teachers of incompetent people.
Incompetent people
are the resources of competent people.
Those who do not value their teachers,
or do not love their resources,
although knowledgeable,
are greatly confused.
This is called the essential detail.

28

Know the male and observe the female
and become the stream of the world.
Be the stream of the world
and the eternal virtue never leaves.
If the eternal virtue never leaves,
then you will return to infancy.

Know the white and observe the black
and be the example for the world.
Be the example for the world
and the eternal virtue never errs.
If the eternal virtue never errs,
then it returns to moderation.

Know the pure and observe the disgrace
and be the valley of the world.
Be the valley of the world
and the eternal virtue will be always enough.
If the eternal virtue is always enough,
then you will return to simplicity.

Simplicity breaks up
and then it becomes tools.
Sages use them and become official leaders.
They will not divide great organisations.

29

If people desire to take the world
and interfere with it,
I see that they have no alternative.
The world is a container of energy
that cannot be interfered with.

Those who act will fail.
Those who hold will lose.
Things may succeed or may fail.
They may be hot or may be cold.
They may be strong or may be weak.
They may grow or may decay.

Therefore, sages
reject extremes,
reject grandeur,
and reject extravagance.

30

Use the Way to assist the leaders of people.
Do not use soldiers to force the world.
Such actions are likely to rebound.
Where armies have camped
only thorny bushes will grow.

Those who are competent
succeed and stop in time.
Do not dare to take power.
Succeed without boasting.
Succeed without attacking.
Succeed without arrogance.
Succeed without excess.
That is called succeeding without force.

Strong things will become weak.
They are not called the Way.
What is not the Way will perish soon.

31

Armies are the tools of misfortune.
They are disgusting.
Therefore, those who possess the Way
will not claim them.

Great men will occupy and value
the unorthodox.
They will use soldiers who value
the orthodox.
Armies are the tools of misfortune.
Therefore, armies
are not the tools of great men.

When there is no alternative then use them.
Attack with sharp weapons
to become victorious,
but use them without satisfaction.
Those who are satisfied by them,
like to kill people.
Those who like to kill people
cannot achieve the goals of the State.
Therefore, during fortunate events,

the left side is honoured.
During funerals,
the right side is honoured.
Therefore, junior generals occupy the left side,
while senior generals occupy the right side.
Their places are determined
in accord with funeral ceremonies.

If people were killed,
then many will attend with sadness.
Hence, treat battle victories
as funeral ceremonies.

32

The Way is forever Nameless.
It is so simple.
Yet, the world should not dare
to control it.

If Marquises and Kings would follow it,
then All-things would submit themselves.
If the Sky and the Earth would unite
with each other,
then it would rain sweet dew.
People would not have to be ordered,
but they would balance themselves.

In an established organisation,
titles will appear.
If titles appear,
then know that it is time to stop.
Know when to stop
and there will be no danger.

The Way is to the world,
what a valley is to a river,
and what a river is to the sea.

33

Those who know other people are wise.
Those who know themselves are brilliant.
Those who overcome
other people have power.
Those who overcome
themselves are strong.
Those who know

what is enough are rich.
Those who are strong pioneers
have ambition.

Those who do not lose their institutions
will last long.
Those who die,
but are not forgotten,
will live on.

34

The Way floats.
It can be unorthodox or orthodox.
It completes its affairs successfully.
Yet, it is not a famous being.
All-things return to it.
Yet, it does not act as their master.
It is always without desire.
Hence, it could be named small.
All-things return to it.
Yet, it does not act as their master.

Hence, it could be named great.
Therefore, sages can achieve greatness,
because they do not act great.
Therefore, they can achieve greatness.

35

Hold on to the Great Image
and the world will come.
It will come
without harm and with great calm.
Music and food
will stop passing travellers.
However, words describing the Way
are called: bland and without taste.

Look at it, and there is not enough to see.
Listen to it, and there is not enough to hear.
However, use it and it cannot be depleted.

36

To fold something,
it must have been unfolded before.
To weaken something,
it must have been strengthened before.
To abandon something,
it must have been attached before.
To seize something,
it must have been separated before.
This is called profound brilliance.

The soft and weak will overcome the strong.
A fish should not leave the deep water.
The sharp weapons of the State
should not be used
in view of the people.

37

The Way is forever Nameless.
If Marquises and Kings could follow it,
then All-things would transform themselves.

If this transformation would cause desire,
then I would suppress it
by using the simplicity of the Nameless.
Suppressing it
by using the simplicity of the Nameless
will not disgrace them.

Use tranquillity without disgrace
and the world will regulate itself.

DE – THE WAY OF PEOPLE

Poems 38—81

38

Superior virtue pursues no virtue.
Therefore, it is virtue.
Inferior virtue pursues virtue.
Therefore, it is no virtue.

Superior virtue uses Non-action
and there is no action used.
Superior benevolence acts
and yet there is no use in those actions.
Superior justice acts
and there is purpose in those actions.
Superior propriety acts
and if there is no agreement,
then the arms are bared.

Therefore, after the Way is lost,
there will be virtue.
After virtue is lost,
there will be benevolence.
After benevolence is lost,
there will be justice.
After justice is lost,
there will be propriety.

Those who have propriety possess
only a thin layer of loyalty and sincerity,
which is the beginning of disorder.
Those who pretend to know the future
are the fruitless flowers of the Way
and the chiefs of fools.

Therefore, great men occupy the thick
and do not occupy the thin.
They occupy the fruit,
but do not occupy the fruitless flowers.
Therefore, reject that and accept this.

39

Of those in the past that obtained the One:
the Sky
obtained the One through pureness;
the Earth
obtained the One through quietness;
the mind
obtained the One through effectiveness;
the valley
obtained the One through filling;
All-things
obtained the One by growing;
and Marquises and Kings
obtained the One by regulating the world.

The conclusion about the One is:
if the Sky is not clear yet,
then fear that it will crack;
if the Earth is not quiet yet,
then fear that it will burst;
if the mind is not effective yet,
then fear that it will cease;
and if the valley is not full yet,
then fear that it will be dry.

If Marquises and Kings
do not use superior nobility,
then fear that they will be overthrown.
Therefore, the noble must use the ignoble
as their foundation.
The high must use the low
as their foundation.
Therefore, Marquises and Kings
call themselves unkindly
'orphans and widowers'.
They use that ignoble foundation incorrectly.
Therefore, they give
too much honour without honour.

Hence, do not desire
the great splendour of jade,
but the grace of natural rock.

40

Returning is the movement of the Way.
Weakness is used by the Way.
The world's things originate from Existence.
Existence originates from Non-existence.

41

If competent scholars hear about the Way,
then they are able to practise it constantly.
If mediocre scholars hear about the Way,
then they put it in a safe place
and seem to lose it.
If incompetent scholars hear about the Way,
then they laugh loudly about it.
If they would not laugh loudly about it,
then they could practice the Way.

Therefore, an established saying states:
"The bright Way seems to be obscure,
the Way forward seems to be backwards,
and the smooth Way seems to be rough."

Superior virtue is just like a valley.
Great pureness seems to be disgrace.
Extensive virtue seems to be insufficient.
Established virtue seems to drift along.
Plain truth seems to change.

The greatest square is without edges.
The greatest talent matures late.
The greatest sound is a rare tone.
The greatest form is shapeless.
The hidden Way is Nameless.
Yet, only the Way is good
at the beginning and good at the end.

42

The Way generated the One.
The One generated the Two.
The Two generated the Three.
The Three generated All-things.

All-things carry Yin on their back
and carry Yang in their arms.
Any difference creates vital energy
that restores their harmony.

People dislike being
unrelated orphans and widowers.
Yet, Kings and Marquises
use those names for themselves.

Things may be harmed by benefit
and may benefit by being harmed.
Therefore, the teachers of humanity
discus and teach people that
violent people will achieve nothing but death.
I will use that as the father of my teachings.

43

The softest of the world
will overcome the hardest of the world.
What is without substance
will penetrate what is without gaps.

Therefore, I know
that there is benefit in Non-action.
Teaching without speaking and Non-action
will benefit the whole world.
Only a few competent people can attain this.

44

Fame or life? What is closer?
Life or wealth? What is worth more?
Gain or loss? What hurts more?

Most people love to spend a lot.
The larger their hoard
the more they have to lose.
Therefore, know what is enough
and there will be no disgrace.
Know when to stop
and there will be no danger.
Accordingly, one will endure long.

45

The greatest achievement
seems to be incomplete.
Yet, its usefulness is not reduced.
The greatest fullness
seems to be empty.
Yet, its usefulness is never exhausted.
The greatest straightness
seems to bend.
The greatest skill
seems clumsy.
The greatest triumph
seems insufficient.

Activity overcomes the cold.
Tranquillity overcomes the heat.
Hence, pure tranquillity can be used
to regulate the world.

46

If the world possesses the Way,
then racehorses will be kept for their manure.
If the world is without the Way,
then warhorses will be bred in the suburbs.

No greater suffering
than having extreme desires.
No greater misfortune
than not knowing what is enough.
No misfortune is more disastrous
than the desire to accumulate.
Therefore, know that enough is enough
and there will be always enough.

47

Do not leave home
in order to learn about the world.
Do not look through the window
in order to learn about the Way of Nature.

The more that people travel far away
the less they know.
Therefore, sages do not travel
and yet they know.
They do not see and yet they name.
They do not act and yet they achieve.

48

Those who daily pursue knowledge
will expand.
Those who daily pursue the Way
will contract.
Contract and contract
until there is Non-action left.
There is no action and yet there is action.

If one wants to take the world,
then one should always use no effort.
When effort is needed,
then there is never enough to take the world.

49

Sages are always without opinions.
They use the opinions of common people
as their opinions.

They are good to those who are good.
They are also good to those who are bad.
So they gain goodness.
They trust those who trust them.
They also trust those who do not trust them.
So they gain trustworthiness.

Sages depend on the world.
Careful, so that they become merged
with the opinion of the world.
All common people focus their ears and eyes.
Instead, all sages are like children.

50

Emerging into life is entering into death.
Three in ten are companions of life.
Three in ten are companions of death.
Three in ten people live extremely
and move into the realm of death.

What is the reason?
That is because they live extremely.
They are incompetent
in hiding, listening, and conserving their lives.

Do not walk through the hills
in order to meet rhinoceroses and tigers.
Do not join the army
in order to carry weapons.

Rhinoceroses have no place
to ram their horns.
Tigers have no place
to strike their claws.
Soldiers have no place
to thrust their swords.

What is the reason?
Because sages avoid the realm of death.

51

The Way generates them
and virtue raises them.
The environment shapes them
and competence completes them.

Therefore, All-things respect the Way
and admire virtue.
Respecting the Way and admiring virtue
is not done to obtain a noble position,
but it is always done to be natural.

The Way generates them and raises them.
It grows them and satisfies them.
It straightens them and matures them.
It supports them and repairs them.

Generate, but do not possess.
Act, but do not rely on it.
Develop but do not exploit.
This is called profound virtue.

52

The beginning of the world
is the Mother of the World.
Obtain the Mother
in order to know her children.
When knowing her children,
return to their nursing Mother,
and produce a life without danger.

Stop the exchange and close the doors;
and to the end of life
there will be no hard work.
Start the exchange and meddle in affairs;
and to the end of life
there will be no safety.

To perceive the small is called brilliant.
Following the soft is called strength.
Use its light to join its brilliance again.
Not losing life to disaster
is called following the constant.

53

Let me have pure knowledge.
When walking on the Great Road,
the only thing scary is action.

The Great Road is very smooth.
Yet, people prefer the narrow winding roads.
Their palaces are very clean.
Their fields are overgrown with weeds.
Their storehouses are very empty.

Those who wear embroidered coloured silk,
carry sharp swords,
gorge on food,
and have a surplus
of goods and resources,
are called 'boasting thieves'.
Boasting thieves are not the Way.

54

Those who establish it competently
cannot be pulled away.
Those who embrace it competently
cannot be separated.
Accordingly, descendants
will pay homage forever.

Cultivate it in yourself
and the virtue will be genuine.
Cultivate it in your household
and its virtue will be plenty.
Cultivate it in your village
and its virtue will last long.
Cultivate it in your country
and its virtue will be abundant.
Cultivate it in the world
and its virtue will be extensive.

Use yourself to examine yourself.
Use households to examine households.
Use villages to examine villages.
Use countries to examine countries.
Use the world to examine the world.

How do I know that the world is like this?
From this account.

55

Those who have substantial virtue
could be compared to new-born babies.
Scorpions, vipers, and insects
do not bite them.
Beasts of prey will not seize them.
Birds of prey will not seize them.

Their bones are weak and their tendons soft.
Yet, their grip is firm.
They do not know
about the joining of male and female.
Yet, their male organ is vigorous.
Their energy is optimal.
They cry all day.
Yet, they do not become hoarse.

Their harmony is optimal.
Knowing harmony is called the constant.
Knowing the constant is called brilliance.
Benefiting life is called fortune.
Using the mind's vital energy
is called powerful.

Strong things will become weak.
They are not called the Way.
What is not the Way will perish soon.

56

Those who know do not speak.
Those who speak do not know.

Stop the exchange
and close the doors.
File their sharpness,
untangle their disorder,
soften their glare,
and merge their dust.

This is called profound unification.
It cannot be achieved by attachment.
Neither can it be achieved by detachment.
It cannot be achieved by benefit.
Neither can it be achieved by harm.
It cannot be achieved by admiration.
Also, it cannot be achieved by contempt.
Therefore, the world admires it.

57

Use justice when ruling the State.
Use surprise when employing armies.
Use no effort when taking the world.
How do I know the world is like this?
Only after this.

The more prohibitions there are in the world,
the poorer the people will be.
The more sharp weapons people have,
the more the State's household
will be confused.
The more people know,
the stranger the things they begin to develop.
Rules increase the content of the law
and, therefore, there will be more criminals.

Therefore, sages have a saying that states:
"I practice Non-action
and the people will transform themselves.
I am tranquil
and the people will perfect themselves.
I use no effort
and the people will become wealthy by
themselves.
I desire not to desire
and the people will become simple by
themselves."

58

If the laws are very lax,
then the people will have extreme surpluses.
If the laws are very strict,
then the people will have extreme shortages
and misfortune.

Misfortune is fortune's place to hide.
Fortune is misfortune's place to hide.
Who knows their extremes?

There is no normal.
Normal turns around and becomes abnormal.
Good turns around and becomes evil.
That has confused everybody for a long time.
Therefore, sages are
interfering but not cutting;
sharp but not stabbing;
straight but not rigid;
and bright but not dazzling.

59

In ruling people and working with nature
there is nothing like frugality.
Only those who are frugal
are called to early service.

Prepare for the call to serve early
by a significant accumulation of virtue.
If there is a significant accumulation of virtue,
then nothing is impossible.
If nothing is impossible,
then one's limits are unknown.
If one's limits are unknown,
then one may possess the country.

Possess the Mother of the Country
and accordingly endure long.
That is called:
having deep roots
and a strong foundation.
Have a long life
through a lasting regard for the Way.

60

Ruling a large country
is like enjoying small delicacies.
Use the Way to attend to the world,
then the underhanded will have no power.
It is not that the underhanded have no power,
but their power will not harm people.
Not that power cannot harm people.
Sages do not harm people either.
Both do not harm each other.
Therefore, virtue unites and returns.

61

A large country should take a low position.
It is the intersection of the world.
It is the female of the world.

The female always uses tranquillity
to overcome the male.
She is tranquil.
Therefore, she is better
in a low position.

Hence, a large country
should use a lower position
than a small country,
when associating with that smaller country.
A small country
should use a lower position
than a large country,
when associating with that larger country.

Therefore, some might take
the lower position to associate.
Others might be in
the lower position to associate.

Those in a large country
only desire to merge and raise people.
Those in a small country
only desire to join other business people.
They all obtain what they desire.
Therefore, the larger one
better acts as the lowest one.

62

People and All-things
concentrate on the Way.
It is the protection
for competent people.
It is the sanctuary
for incompetent people.

Pleasing words
might be exchanged.
Respectful conduct
might honour people.
Incompetent people forsake
their Existence unnecessarily.

Therefore, when the Emperor is crowned
and the three ministers are installed,
a millstone of jade preceded by four horses,
is not as good as sitting down
and presenting this.

So, why did the Ancients value
the protection of the Way?
Did they not say:
"Use it to obtain what you seek
and use it to escape what you suffer."
Therefore, it is valuable for the whole world.

63

Act with Non-action.
Work without effort.
Taste without savouring.
Make the large small and the many few.
Repay hatred with kindness.
Pursue the difficult, while it is easy.
Act large, while it is still small.

The world's most difficult things
arise from the easiest.
The world's largest things
arise from the smallest.
Therefore, all sages
will avoid great actions.
Hence, they can achieve greatness.

Those who make rash promises
are certainly difficult to trust.
Those who regard everything as easy
will have certainly many difficulties.
Therefore, sages regard everything as difficult.
Hence, they have no difficulties in the end.

64

That what is at rest is easy to hold.
That what is not manifest is easy to plan.
That what is fragile is easy to break.
That what is small is easy to scatter.
Act when it has not happened yet.
Control it when it is not chaotic yet.

A tree that takes both arms to embrace
grows from a little cutting.
Nine-tenth of a tower
rises from a simple basket of earth.
A thousand meters height
starts from under your feet.

Those who act will fail.
Those who hold will lose.
Therefore, sages will use Non-action.
Therefore, they will not fail.
They will not hold.
Therefore, they will not lose.

In handling their affairs,
people fail often close to their success.
Therefore, be as careful at the end
as at the beginning.
Then affairs will not fail.

Therefore, sages desire not to desire
and do not admire goods
that are difficult to obtain.
They learn not to learn
and repair the mistakes of others.
Sages complement the nature of all All-things,
but they do not dare to act.

65

Therefore, the Ancients said:
"Do not use the Way of Action
to enlighten people."
Instead, use their simplicity.
People are difficult to rule
if they use their knowledge.

Therefore, using knowledge
to rule the country
is betraying the country.
Using no knowledge
to rule the country
is benefiting the country.
Remember always those two things.

Examine also the principle.
Always remembering to examine the principle
is called profound virtue.
Profound virtue is deep.
Even far away things return to it.
The great order is perfect.

66

How are the river and the sea able
to be the Kings of a hundred valleys?
They use competently their low position.
Therefore, they are able
to be Kings of a hundred valleys.
Therefore, sages who
desire to be above the people
must place themselves below them.

Those who desire to lead people
must place themselves behind them.
Therefore, they stay above
and the people will not weight them down.
They stay in front
and the people will not harm them.

Everyone in the world
will be happy to elect them
without objections.
Having no purpose, they do not strive.
Therefore the world cannot strive with them.

67

Everyone in the world calls me great.
Great and different.
Only those who are different can be great.
If they were similar,
then they would be insignificant.

I have always three treasures
that I keep and protect.
The first one is called compassion.
The second one is called frugality.
The third one is called humbleness.

Those who are compassionate
can be courageous.
Those who are frugal
can be generous.
Those who are humble
can be successful leaders of affairs.

Now, those who
abandon compassion and are yet courageous;
abandon their frugality and are yet generous;
abandon their humbleness and are yet leading;
they will certainly die.

Those who use compassion to attack
will triumph.
Those who use it to defend
will stand firm.
Nature will protect them
with a wall of compassion.

68

Competent warriors do not like war.
Competent chiefs will not get angry.
Competent conquerors will not engage.
Competent leaders will take a low position.

That is called the virtue of not striving.
That is called employing people.
That is called matching with nature.
It is the ultimate principle of the Ancients.

69

Warriors have a saying that states:
"I do not dare to act as a host,
but act as a guest.
I do not dare to advance an inch,
but retreat a foot."
That is called:
moving without moving.
Rolling up the sleeves
without showing an arm.

Be without resistance.
Hold without weapons.
No greater misfortune
than meeting no resistance.
Meeting no resistance
is close to losing my treasures.
Therefore, when equal armies face each other
the reluctant one will win.

70

My words are very easy to understand
and very easy to apply.
Yet, people cannot understand them
and they cannot apply them.

My words have precedence
and my affairs have a sovereign,
but they do not understand that.
Therefore, they do not understand me.
I am valuable to those few
who understand me.
Therefore, sages wear cheap cloth
that conceals jade.

71

Knowing that you do not know
earns respect.
Not knowing that you do not know
is a weakness.
Therefore, sages are not weak.
They consider their weakness as a weakness.
Hence, it is not a weakness.

72

When people do not fear authority,
then greater authority will appear.
Do not take their dwellings by force.
Do not reject them a place to live.
Only, if they are not rejected,
they will not reject you.

Sages know themselves,
but do not display themselves.
They love themselves,
but do not admire themselves.
Therefore, reject that and accept this.

73

Those who are courageous in daring
will be killed.
Those who are courageous in not daring
will live.
Those two things
could be beneficial or could be harmful.

Nature takes a low place.
Who knows its reason?
The Way of Nature is not to strive,
but to overcome through competence.
Without speaking,
it answers with competence.
Without calling,
things come.
It is simple and plans with competence.
The net of nature is very extensive.
It dredges and nothing escapes.

74

If people never fear death,
how could the use of executions scare them?
If people always fear death and act abnormal,
how could I dare to seize,
hold, and execute them?

If people always fear certain death,
then there is always someone
in charge of executing them.
Those who act on behalf of the one
that is in charge of the executions,
execute as if they act
on behalf of the Master Carpenter.
From those who act
on behalf of the Master Carpenter
only a few will not cut their hands.

75

People are hungry,
because their food taxes are high.
Therefore, they are hungry.
Common people cannot be governed,
because their leaders act
for their own purposes.
Therefore, the people cannot be governed.

People take death lightly,
because they seek to live substantially.
Therefore, they take death lightly.
Only those who do not act
for the purpose of living
are knowledgeable at valuing life.

76

People are born soft and weak.
They die, hard and strong.
All-things, grasses, and trees
are born soft and fragile.
They die, dry and brittle.

Therefore, the hard and strong
are called companions of death.
The soft and weak
are the companions of life.
Hence, a strong army will not win.
A strong tree will be broken.

Therefore, the strong and big
occupy the low positions.
The soft and weak
occupy the high positions.

77

The Way of Nature is like flexing a bow.
High things are lowered.
Low things are raised.
It takes from those who have plenty.
It gives to those who have not enough.
Therefore, it is the Way of Nature
to take from what is plenty
and give to what is not enough.

However, the Way of People is different.
They take from what is not enough
and give to what is plenty.
Hence, those who have plenty and give
to those in the world who have not enough
are the only ones who possess the Way.
Therefore, sages act, but do not rely on it.
They succeed, but do not claim.
They do not desire to display their knowledge.

78

Nothing in the world
is as soft and weak as water.
Yet, in attacking hard and strong things,
nothing has a greater ability
to overcome them.
Therefore, nothing could replace its purpose.

The softest will overcome the hardest.
The weakest will overcome the strongest.
Nobody in the world does not know this.
Yet, nobody does practise it.

Therefore, sages have a saying that states:
"Accept the country's shame
and be called the Kingdom's leader.
Accept the country's misfortune
and be called the world's King."
True words seem to be paradoxical.

79

Calm a great hate
and certainly some hate will remain.
How could this be considered competent?

Therefore, sages
adhere to orthodox agreements
and do not obligate other people by purpose.
Therefore, those with virtue
will uphold the agreement.
Those without virtue
will uphold the details.

The Way of Nature has no favourites.
It is always with the competent people.

80

In a small country with a few people,
let everybody have many tools,
but not use them.
Let the people be serious about death
and not move far away.
Let them have carriages
without using them.
Let them have weapons
without displaying them.
Let them return to knotted cords
and use them.

Sweeten their food
and beautify their clothes.
Enjoy their customs
and secure their dwellings.

Neighbouring countries
will see each other in the distance.
They hear each other's chickens and dogs.
Nevertheless, the people die of old age
and have never visited each other.

81

True words are not pleasing.
Pleasing words are not true.
Those who know are not educated.
Those who are educated do not know.
Those who are competent have not much.
Those who have much are not competent.

Sages do not hoard.
Since they are used to act for other people,
they receive more possessions for themselves.
Since they are used to give to other people,
they have much more themselves.

The Way of Nature
is beneficial and without harm.
Accordingly, the Way of People
should be action without strive.

THE SCIENCE OF LIVING

Any literal translation of *Dao De Jing* will still hide the true meaning of Lao Zi's philosophy behind his ancient terminology and holistic way of thinking. Therefore, the meaning of his poems is explained in (Schade, Stunning Revelations about Lao Zi's Dao De Jing, 2017).

Those revelations show that Lao Zi applies theoretical physics to psychology. That makes sense, because if one knows the principle of nature, then one knows also the principle for living. After all, a goldfish living in a spherical bowl is forced to swim in circles. The shape of the bowl determines the behaviour of the fish. The fish has to know the principle of the bowl in order to have a long life with a minimum of effort.

Similarly, human behaviour is conditioned by nature to follow the laws of physics. Those laws are predictable, because they are the result of Lao Zi's principle of the dynamic yin-yang balances constituting our reality. To succeed within that system of balances, sages have to be humble, efficient, and proactive. They will not rock the boat; they go with the flow; and will prevent, rather than cure (Schade, Stunning Revelations about Lao Zi's Dao De Jing, 2017).

On the surface, Lao Zi's beautiful poems are about the art of living. They seem to be about the heart, rather than the head. However, he warned you—*My words are very easy to understand and very easy to apply. Yet, people cannot understand them and they cannot apply them [70].* On a deeper level, those poems are about the science of living, because the immutable laws of nature determine how you could live long with a minimum of effort. Lao Zi synthesizes the heart and the head. As a result, his poems are about the scientific art of living.

APPENDIX

DR. AUKE SCHADE

My life started during the devastation of World War II. As a teenager, I worked as a carpenter and studied building engineering at night school. During the seventies, I became a financial manager for a multinational corporation, ran my own business, and studied economics in my spare time. My interest in the psychology of management extended to the interaction between the mind, body, and reality. In 1980, I immigrated to New Zealand where I obtained a doctorate in psychology from the University of Auckland. My mission is to make people the smartest thinkers they can be, which has led me to the development of (Schade A. , Think Smarter with Nemonik Thinking., 2016)

BIBLIOGRAPHY

Bodde, D. (1983). *Fung Yu-lan: A History of Chinese Philosophy*. Princeton University Press, Princeton.

Schade, A. (2018). *Dictionary Lao Zi's Dao De Jing* (1 ed., Vol. 1). nemonik-thinking.org.

Schade, A. (2018). *Lao Tzu's Tao Te Ching (English)* (2 ed.). nemonik-thinking.org.

Schade, A. (2018). *Lao Zi's Dao De Jing (Chinese-English)* (2 ed.). nemonik-thinking.org.

Schade, A. (2017). *Lao Zi's Dao De Jing Demystified* (2 ed., Vol. 4). nemonik-thinking.org.

Schade, A. (2017). *Lao Zi's Dao De Jing for Nemonik Thinkers* (2 ed.). nemonik-thinking.org.

Schade, A. (2018). *Lao Zi's Poems (large print)* (1 ed.). nemonik-thinking.org.

Schade, A. (2018). *Lao Zi's Poems* (1 ed.). nemonik-thinking.org.

Schade, A. (2018). *Meta-translation Lao Zi's Dao De Jing (1-37)* (3 ed., Vol. 2). nemonik-thinking.org.

Schade, A. (2018). *Meta-translation Lao Zi's Dao De Jing (38-81)* (3 ed., Vol. 3). nemonik-thinking.org.

Schade, A. (2017). *Stunning Revelations about Lao Zi's Dao De Jing* (2 ed., Vol. 5). nemonik-thinking.org.

Schade, A. (2016). *Think Smarter with Nemonik Thinking*. (3 ed.). nemonik-thinking.org.

Schade, A. (2016). *Think Smarter with Nemonik Thinking*. nemonik-thinking.org.

GLOSSARY

Antimatter—See Non-existence.

Dao (道)—means literally road, path, way, or pathway. However, in the context of Lao Zi's philosophy, Dao means the Way of Nature. Lao Zi's Way of Nature is the principle, substance, and force of the universe that explains the origin, formation, and working of the universe. The three main characteristics of the Way of Nature are Oneness, Nothingness, and Infiniteness. Nowadays, the study of the Way of Nature is called Physics. Lao Zi's Way of Nature is the highest of his Four Greatnesses that constitute the universe. However, it has so many manifestations that it cannot be given a single name. For example, water can manifest itself as ice or steam, but its true essence remains water. Similarly, the Way of Nature has different manifestations, but its true essence remains the Way of Nature. It may manifest itself as a soft rain on a summer afternoon, a spinning electron, lightening, a tornado, an earthquake, a waterfall, a supernova, a black-hole and so on. Hence, Lao Zi uses many synonyms and metaphors to describe the manifestations of the Way of Nature such as: Constant, Desolate, Empty, Father of the Multitude, Great Image, Great Road, Immortal Valley Spirit, Infiniteness, Master Carpenter, Mother, Mysterious Female, Named, Nameless Oneness, Nameless, Nothingness, One, River, Simplicity, Valley, Vital Energy, and Water. Furthermore, the Way of Nature is bound to maintain the cosmological constancy of Nothingness. Therefore, the Way of Nature becomes clearly detectable as the force Qi during the restoration of Yin-Yang balances. Dao is a phonetic notation of a Chinese pictograph and, therefore, it is alternatively spelled as Tao.

De (德)—means literally virtue. However, within the context of Lao Zi's Dao De Jing; De (德) is the opposite of Dao (道). Dao is the Way of Nature or Physics. Hence, De is the Way of People or Psychology. De is a phonetic notation for the Chinese pictograph (德), which is alternatively spelled as Te.

Efficiency—See Non-action.

Eternal downward force—See Immortal Valey Sprit.

Existence or Matter (有)—everything that we can perceive in the collective-sensory reality and that is the equal opposite of Non-existence.

Gravity—See Immortal Valey Sprit.

Immortal Valley Spirit (谷神不死)—Lao Zi's beautiful poetic term has a modern scientific meaning. The pictographs 不死 …immortal… could be replaced with the synonym …eternal… Furthermore, 谷 …valley… is a metaphor for …downward… The rain water flows downwards from the top of the mountain along the walls of the valley towards the lowest point at the bottom of the valley. The secular meaning for 神 …spirit… is 神 …force… Consequently, Lao Zi's 谷神不死 …Immortal Valley Spirit… could be called …Eternal Downward Force…, which is a scientific definition of gravity. See Mysterious Female.

Matter—See Existence.

Mysterious Female—(玄牝)—Lao Zi's term for Gravity. See Immortal Valey Sprit.

Non-action or Efficiency (无 为)—means literally *action without action*. The principle of

Non-action entails an efficient use of the unlimited force of the Way of Nature so that sages achieve their goals with a minimum of effort and resources.

Non-existence or Antimatter(无 or 无有)— hypothetical concept introduced by Lao Zi that cannot be perceived directly in the collective-sensory reality and is the equal opposite of Existence.

Physics—See Dao.

Psychology—See De.

The Way of Nature—See Dao.

The Way of People—See De.

MY OTHER BOOKS

Dictionary Lao Zi's *Dao De Jing* [1 of 5].

This Chinese-English and English-Chinese dictionary is especially compiled for the translation of Lao Zi's ancient book Dao De Jing (Schade, Meta-translation Lao Zi's Dao De Jing (1-37), 2018) and (Schade, Meta-translation Lao Zi's Dao De Jing (38-81), 2018).   Dao De Jing means literally—A Classic about the Way of Nature and the Way of People. It aims to maximize your success, which is to obtain what you seek and escape what you suffer.   Success is maximized by aligning the Way of People with the Way of Nature (Schade, Stunning Revelations about Lao Zi's Dao De Jing, 2017). The Chinese versions used in this study include— (Wang Bi, 226-249 AD); (He-Shang Gong, 179-157 BC); (Fu Yi, ~200 BC); (Mawangdui (A), ~200 BC); (Mawangdui (B), ~200 BC); and (Guodian, ~300 BC).   Together, those versions contain about 1,600 different pictographs. Every language changes over time and, therefore, some of Lao Zi's ancient pictographs are not used anymore, while the meaning of others has changed. In addition, most modern Chinese pictographs have several English meanings that foster ambiguity. Therefore, the exhaustive English meanings for each pictograph were extracted from reputable sources. Furthermore, a system of Digital Index for Pictographs (DIP) is introduced that simplifies the digital classification of Chinese pictographs.

Free eBook @
nemonik-thinking.org

Meta-translation Lao Zi's *Dao*... [2 of 5]

The title of Lao Zi's ancient book Dao De Jing means literally—A Classic about the Way of Nature and the Way of People. Dao De Jing aims to maximize your success, which is to obtain what you seek and escape what you suffer. Success is maximized by aligning the Way of People with the Way of Nature (Schade, Stunning Revelations about Lao Zi's Dao De Jing, 2017). Despite the great efforts, previous translations of Dao De Jing do not present an adequate understanding of that mysterious manuscript. In order to take optimal advantage of the expertise accumulated in such earlier studies, this meta-translation is based on an English meta-analysis and a Chinese meta-analysis. The English meta-analysis is based on the following English translations— (Chan Wing-Tsit, 1988); (Cheng Gia-Fu and English, J, 1972); (Henricks, Lao-Tzu: Te-Tao Ching, 1993); (Land, 1990); (Lau, Lao Tzu: Tao Te Ching, 1985); (Lin, J. P., 1977); (Man-ho Kwok; Palmer, M.; & Ramsay, J., 1997); (Waley, 1968); and (Wing, 1986). The Chinese meta-analysis is based on the following Chinese versions of Dao De Jing—

(Wang Bi, 226-249 AD); (He-Shang Gong, 179-157 BC); (Fu Yi, ~200 BC); (Mawangdui (A), ~200 BC); (Mawangdui (B), ~200 BC); and (Guodian, ~300 BC). This meta-translation of Dao (Chapters 1-37) is based on a special dictionary (Schade, Dictionary Lao Zi's Dao De Jing, 2018), while it is the foundation for (Schade, Lao Zi's Dao De Jing Demystified, 2017).

Free eBook @
nemonik-thinking.org

Meta-translation Lao Zi's *Dao...* [3 of 5]

The title of Lao Zi's ancient book Dao De Jing means literally—A Classic about the Way of Nature and the Way of People. Dao De Jing aims to maximize your success, which is to obtain what you seek and escape what you suffer. Success is maximized by aligning the Way of People with the Way of Nature (Schade, Stunning Revelations about Lao Zi's Dao De Jing, 2017). Despite the great efforts, previous translations of Dao De Jing do not present an adequate understanding of that mysterious manuscript. In order to take optimal advantage of the expertise accumulated in such earlier studies, this meta-translation is based on an English meta-analysis and a Chinese meta-analysis. The English meta-analysis is based on the following English translations— (Chan Wing-Tsit, 1988); (Cheng Gia-Fu and English, J, 1972); (Henricks, Lao-Tzu: Te-Tao Ching, 1993); (Land, 1990); (Lau, Lao Tzu: Tao Te Ching, 1985); (Lin, J. P., 1977); (Man-ho Kwok; Palmer, M.; & Ramsay, J., 1997); (Waley, 1968); and (Wing, 1986). The Chinese meta-analysis is based on the following Chinese versions of Dao De Jing—

(Wang Bi, 226-249 AD); (He-Shang Gong, 179-157 BC); (Fu Yi, ~200 BC); (Mawangdui (A), ~200 BC); (Mawangdui (B), ~200 BC); and (Guodian, ~300 BC). This meta-translation of De (Chapters 38-81) is based on a special dictionary (Schade, Dictionary Lao Zi's Dao De Jing, 2018), while it is the foundation for (Schade, Lao Zi's Dao De Jing Demystified, 2017).

Free eBook @
nemonik-thinking.org

Lao Zi's *Dao De Jing* Demystified [4 of 5]

The title of Lao Zi's ancient book Dao De Jing means literally—A Classic about the Way of Nature and the Way of People. It aims to maximize your success, which is to obtain what you seek and escape what you suffer. Success is maximized by aligning the Way of People with the Way of Nature. The current study presents four English versions of increasing demystification. The first one is the Meta-translation version as developed in (Schade, Meta-translation Lao Zi's Dao De Jing (1-37), 2018) and (Schade, Meta-translation Lao Zi's Dao De Jing (38-81), 2018). However, Lao Zi's poetic style, mysticism, metaphors, and synonyms are still inhibiting a clear understanding. The second one is the Clarification version, which is presented in parallel with the Meta-translation. That clarification increased the consistency of Lao Zi's terminology, but significant chapters about Dao are still located in the De section and vice versa. Therefore, the third one is the Chapters Reorganized version in which the chapters are relocated to the Dao and De sections. Nevertheless, the text remains fuzzy, because several chapters relate to both sections. Therefore, the fourth one is the Sentences Reorganized version in which the sentences are sorted by topic. That version is the foundation for (Schade, Stunning Revelations about Lao Zi's Dao De Jing, 2017).

Free eBook @ nemonik-thinking.org

Stunning Revelations about Lao Zi... [5 of 5]

The title of Lao Zi's ancient book Dao De Jing means in modern terminology—A Classic about the Physics of Psychology. Dao De Jing is a significant contribution of the Chinese literature to the contemporary sciences of physics and psychology. Lao Zi presents a sophisticated theory concerning the origin, formation, and working of the universe. Although that theory is at the cutting edge of modern physics, it provides a simple and practical principle. That principle holds that the unstoppable force Qi will always maintain the multitude of Yin-Yang balances comprising our universe. Therefore, Lao Zi's theory of psychology predicts that people can only maximize their success by aligning with Qi. Success is to obtain what you seek and escape what you suffer. Unfortunately, humanity has ignored Lao Zi's principles for two-and-halve thousand years. As a result, we are now facing manmade problems such as climate change, continuous warfare, dwindling resources, environmental pollution, and overpopulation. Those problems threaten your personal success and they cannot be solved with the same way of thinking that has created them. Therefore, Lao Zi's Dao De Jing is more relevant than ever. His way of dynamic thinking fosters solutions that reach peacefully across the fault-lines created by race, religion, and ideology. This book is based on (Schade, Lao Zi's Dao De Jing Demystified, 2017).

Free eBook @
nemonik-thinking.org

Think Smarter with Nemonik Thinking

Nemonik thinking will improve your life. It accelerates your thinking; improves your memory; mobilizes your subconscious genius; strengthens your weaknesses; and reveals opportunities and threats. It helps you to pursue your goals in the right state of mind; at the right place, at the right time, with the right resources; and the right information. Nemonik thinking will assist you to think on your feet and become panic resistant during emergencies. Nemonik thinking is simple to learn, but it so sophisticated that it will make you a superior problem solver. Nemonik thinkers evaluate a checklist of seventeen nemoniks for each situation. Nemoniks are memorized keywords describing all aspects of your mind, reality, and their interaction. Nemonik thinking is like playing a musical keyboard with seventeen keys producing an infinite repertoire of practical strategies. Nemonik thinking provides the strategic options for any possible situation, while Lao Zi's Dao De Jing provides the principle that identifies which of those options will fit the actual situation (Schade, Stunning Revelations about Lao Zi's Dao De Jing, 2017). The resulting strategies will maximize your success, which is to obtain what you seek and escape what you suffer. You might be the best thinker in the world, but only nemonik thinking could make you the smartest thinker you can be.

Free eBook @
nemonik-thinking.org

WEBSITE

It is the aim of my website to provide interactive on-line information about nemonik thinking. This includes discussions, books, blog, videos, exercises, updates, activities, web links, and tests. Join the nemonik thinkers and receive the latest updates. It is a work in progress. Check it out and have your say! I look forward to your feedback at:

nemonik-thinking.org